Around Penrith

IN OLD PHOTOGRAPHS

The Round-about, Devonshire Street, 1815. The very ancient building on the left was called the Round-about. There were two shops on the first floor and butchers stood with their meat all around the building; next came two rows of fishstones. This view of the building is from an oil painting by local artist Jacob Thompson belonging to the Hutton family. The Round-about was eventually sold by public auction in the Market Place on 27 May 1826. The Moot Hall, Shambles and the Cross appear to have been removed around 1809. The *Penrith Observer* of 16 November 1897 names some of the characters depicted in the painting, including on the left, old Martin, a razor grinder, Jack Graham, a noted angler, and Tommy Dawson, town crier, who was also sexton of St Andrew's church (extreme right).

Around Penrith

IN OLD PHOTOGRAPHS

Collected by FRANK BOYD

ALAN SUTTON

Alan Sutton Publishing Limited
Phoenix Mill · Far Thrupp · Stroud
Gloucestershire

**British Library Cataloguing
in Publication Data**

Boyd, Frank
  Around Penrith in Old Photographs
  I. Title
  942.786

  ISBN 0-7509-0281-7

Typeset in 9/10 Sabon
Typesetting and origination by
Alan Sutton Publishing Limited.
Printed in Great Britain by
Redwood Books, Trowbridge.

First published 1993

Contents

Introduction

Because of my great interest in photography, and my affection for the town of Penrith, where I was born and bred, it has given me much pleasure to compile this book.

It would have been impossible, however, without the generous help of many kind friends who have searched out and lent to me numerous old treasured photographs in their possession, and have been unstinting in passing on to me not only the personal memories evoked but also information which supplemented my photographs and research.

The fascinating story of Penrith down the ages, from its early beginnings in the tenth century as capital of Cumbria, then as part of the kingdom of Scotland, up to the present day, is touched upon in these pages. Now Penrith is an expanding, flourishing market town of charm and beauty, its important position at the gateway to the Lake District adding prestige and prosperity.

Many of the people who bring history to life wander through this book. I hope older readers will experience the warmth of glad recognition, and younger ones will learn of those who have gone before and helped to build their historic home town into so vital and desirable a place.

SECTION ONE
Market Place

Crowds celebrate Queen Victoria's Golden Jubilee on 23 June 1887 in Penrith's busiest street, the Market Place. No one ventured out without a hat in those days – even in summer.

Celebrating the Queen's Diamond Jubilee in 1897. In the foreground are soldiers and the mounted band of the Westmorland and Cumberland Yeomanry. On the left of the picture in the background can be seen the fire-engine and its brass helmeted firemen.

A farmer and his wife arrive in town by horse and cart on another busy Tuesday in 1904.

Market day around the same time, with farmers' carts parked on the side of the steet, the horses having been stabled behind the hotels. Thos Altham's shop at the time was on the right hand side of the market arcade.

Market Place from another angle around 1904. On the right is Canton House, the grocery store of the Hetherington Brothers. Mrs Elizabeth Hetherington, grandmother to the three brothers, Tom, Dick and Alf, ran her own shop (to the right of the monument) until she was 82.

In the early 1900s the George Hotel was the largest and most central hotel in town. For many generations the property of the Dukes of Devonshire, it passed into the hands of Mr Fred Armstrong in December 1892. Ullswater coaches left here four times daily during the season. Next door the London and North Western Railway Company had a parcel receiving office.

The focal point of Penrith's busy Market Place, as it was known in the early days (now Market Square and Devonshire Street), is the fine Musgrave monument and clock tower. On its north side it bears the inscription, 'In sympathy with the great sorrow which befell the family at Edenhall in the death of their eldest son, Phillip Musgrave Esq on May 16th, 1859, at Madrid, in the 26th year of his age, this monument was erected, May 1861. A tribute from the town and neighbourhood of their high regard and esteem for Sir George and Lady Musgrave.' For several centuries the Musgrave family took a prominent part in the life and affairs of Cumberland and Westmorland. This view shows Market Square and Devonshire Street in around 1910. Penrith's first telephone exchange operated from the high building on the left, where two roof-top aerials may be seen.

A wintry scene. On the right of the picture is one of Penrith's oldest shops, James and John Graham's, established in 1793. As well as being grocers and provision merchants, the sign above the shop informs us they employed Italian warehousemen.

The well-stocked interior of the Market Square shop of J. & J. Graham's in 1905. A 97-page booklet was published in response to numerous requests from customers at that time, containing an alphabetical list of goods kept in stock.

A large crowd assembled near the monument on a busy market day. The block comprising the Bank of Liverpool and Bowerbank's Ironmongers was demolished in 1912. The *Advertiser* office and the YMCA remained.

This picture shows the new-style Bank of Liverpool after being rebuilt and incorporating Bowerbank's, thus leaving only ground floor premises for Bowerbank & Son. The new bank reopened for business under the management of Mr J.H. Bates on 21 July 1913. It changed to Liverpool & Martins in 1918 and was shortened to Martins in 1928. It is now Barclay's.

For many years the focal point of Penrith has been its handsome memorial to a son of the Musgrave family. The busy scene depicted shows that here was the hub of the town. To the left stands the beautiful building of the London City & Midland Bank completed in 1913. The photograph was taken on 29 July of that year. To the right a wagonette drawn by three horses and packed with a crowd of holiday-makers has just set off from the George Hotel.

The centre of Penrith after the Midland Bank replaced Clark's Butchers and Thompson's Ironmongers in 1913. In 1923 Messrs Glassons sold the adjoining Devonshire Inn, with its old established wine and spirit business, to the Midland Bank. The inn was pulled down and the Bank built an addition to their premises on the site.

The high standing of the George Hotel, seen here in the 1920s with its array of window boxes and hanging baskets, is demonstrated by three chauffeur-driven landaus awaiting guests.

Penrith is now an important market town where much business is transacted. Here in 1922 two of several new banks are shown, the Midland and the National Provincial. At the north end of Devonshire Street stands the shop of N. Arnison & Sons, Drapers, Costumiers and Milliners. Penrith's oldest established business, it celebrated its 250th anniversary in 1992. Arnison's shop is a listed seventeenth-century building and was originally built as a fine residence for a wealthy Penrith family. Its most famous residents were William and Ann Cookson, the maternal grandparents of William Wordsworth.

Tom Smith's shop. The only bit of old Penrith in Devonshire Street that the process of industrial and commercial development has not altered is the shop owned by Mr Tom Smith, grocer. Although renovated, the shop-front retains its original character.

Henry Clark & Son, butchers, established in 1830, was, at the beginning of the century, situated next to the Devonshire Hotel. Now just a few doors away, it retains its high reputation as a family butchers. In 1847 there were fourteen butchers in the town.

Market Hall, Devonshire Street, *c.* 1912. The first portion was built in 1860, and the second in 1866 at a cost of £12,000. Prior to its erection markets were held in the streets: butter and fruit in Devonshire Street, poultry in Burrowgate, the potato market in Middlegate, pork and wool in Great Dockray, live pigs and sheep in Sandgate. The Corn Exchange still keeps the open street in Cornmarket. Penrith Market Hall was once more important than its name implies, as everything from the annual washerwoman's ball to concerts, election meetings and lectures were held here during its Victorian heyday.

The Town

Cornmarket, so called because busy farmers came in from the country with their horses and carts to the Corn Exchange to buy agricultural implements, butter churns, and other useful goods. The granite trough was where thirsty horses could drink from. The trough is now to be found in the Castle Park, inscribed 'In memory of Lucy Waring Varty of Stagstones, Penrith, 1897'. Kerr's fruit shop, on the right, has moved across to where the old White Hart Hotel was. Edmondson's chemist retains its original position having been established in 1726. Other shops are still there. This photograph was taken around 1904.

Just round the corner in Market Square, shop assistants pose for the cameraman at the premises of Harold Thompson, tin-plate worker, brazier, coppersmith and general ironmonger. Next door is Miss Sarah Birkett's small shop selling children's clothes. The whole block was eventually demolished and rebuilt by the Midland Bank. Thompson's moved to the bottom of Castlegate with its workshop further up the hill.

Hetherington Brothers' drapery and grocers shops stand where the Griffin Inn was before being demolished in the early 1890s. The host of the inn for several years was William Jameson, a champion wrestler. On the upper part of the building is listed all the commodities on offer in the store. This is now the NORWEB shop. The White Hart Hotel on the right is just visible. It is mentioned as early as 1720 and was closed in 1922. William Kerr, florist and fruiterer, bought the property, moving in from the opposite side of the square.

A view of Cornmarket taken ten years later, at the beginning of the First World War. Note the early motor car.

John Pearson's pork butcher's shop at No. 11 Cornmarket, with the staff who have decorated the premises for the festive season in 1910. The attractive array of plates, festooned with holly, bear the greetings 'A Merry Christmas', 'A Happy New Year', and 'A Hearty Welcome'. Ham shanks, sausages and pies are displayed for sale. It is interesting to note that the building dates from 1624 and is still there today.

The Church Army fulfilling its missionary work has drawn a large crowd of worshippers in Cornmarket, Penrith, about 1912. Two horse and carts stand outside the Gloucester Arms Hotel.

Great Dockray, *c.* 1895. Prior to the erection of the Market Hall the market for pork and wool was held in Great Dockray. In the centre was a small kiosk, which sold sweets and cigarettes. Inside, at one time, was a large stone with a ring on top, originally used in bull baiting and kept as a memento. The last tenants of the kiosk were Mr and Mrs Harrison, until 1942, when the kiosk was damaged by a lorry and later demolished. Outside the kiosk was the weighbridge, which was constantly in use. A large sack of wool can be seen beside the kiosk in the photograph. The bull-baiting arena in the early nineteenth century was in the courtyard of the Two Lions Hotel, the well-to-do and the poor alike taking part in it. Eventually Edwin Grave and William Varty were instrumental in putting an end to this brutal sport. Cock fighting was also much practised. Both events were sometimes staged on Sundays in Sandgate, too. The Two Lions, built in 1585, had at one time been residence of Gerard Lowther.

Another view of Great Dockray, again on market day, in the 1930s, this time looking towards Cornmarket and Castlegate, with the kiosk very prominent in the foreground. In the distance is Pattinson and Winter's old mill, now converted into flats and offices. The 65 ft chimney was demolished in 1936. At the foot of Castlegate can be seen the Fish Hotel, which was built in about 1812 and demolished in 1972.

Dockray Hall (now the Gloucester Arms) was built in 1580 and is closely associated with Penrith Castle, being the residence of Ralph Neville, who built the castle. It is said that there was a subterranean passage between the Hall and the castle, the entrance and exit having long since disappeared, although a place in the hotel cellar is still regarded as a probable opening. The sign above the door is a copy of the arms of Richard III, who bore the name 'Haunchback'. He resided for some time at Dockray Hall and the castle.

Vast crowds of people thronged Great Dockray on Whit Tuesday in the 1950s, when the fair arrived with its merry-go-rounds, side-shows and stalls, one of the most popular of which was the coconut-shy. Walter Harney and his wife were regular visitors for many years with their 'Roll your Penny Stall'.

This flourishing Family Temperance Hotel in Cornmarket, advertising 'good stabling and accommodation for cycles', was run by Mrs N. Borrowdale, whose son Tommy became one of the town's 'characters'. She is seen here in the doorway with some of her staff around the turn of the century. It has changed hands several times and been modernized and is now a gown shop.

Looking up Castlegate in the early 1950s, with the Fish Hotel, which was demolished in 1972 on the right, and Tommy Dayson's snack-bar on the opposite corner. Before the Second World War, H. Thompson, ironmonger, occupied this shop, and in May 1942 it was opened by the YMCA as a serviceman's canteen.

Just above the Fish on the right was the chemist's shop of Francis Crowden, seen here standing in the doorway about the turn of the century. Mr Crowden registered as a chemist and druggist on 15 April 1874. At that time there were nine druggists in Penrith. The large bottles full of coloured liquid which were popular in chemists at that time can be seen in the windows, and various sizes of sponges are for sale — 'Splendid value at only 6d each'.

Castlegate around 1895. The raised portion of footpath, the steps on the right, and a shorter length of raised footpath further up the street existed until the late 1920s. The furniture and upholstery shop in the right foreground belonged to Mrs C. Douglas. J. Wood kept the Temperance Hotel. It is interesting to note that there were at least five temperance hotels in Castlegate at this time. In front of the horse and trap is the workshop of H. Thompson, ironmonger, whose shop was where the Midland Bank now stands in Market Square.

A bustling Castlegate in 1904, the roadway full of pedestrians heading down towards the Cornmarket, passing Sissons Temperance Hotel, A. Strong, Confectioner and Tea Rooms, and Oglethorpe's Drapers. The raised portion of the footpath can be seen on the left of the picture.

A sunny day in June 1932 as horse and float gaily decorated with roses and carrying Rose Queen Winnie Norman and her attendants leads the Sons of Temperance procession up Castlegate. Back row, left to right: Annie Thompson, Winnie Norman, Doris Rose. Front row: Bertha Stephenson, Dick Pickering and Betty Hartness.

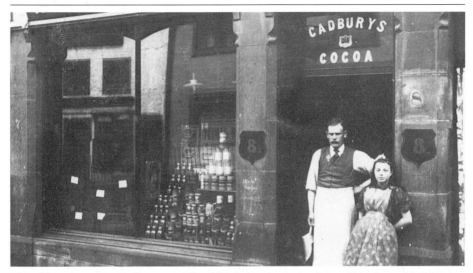

This old picture of 1905 shows Mr Thos Thistlethwaite at the door of his shop with Margaret Marrs, daughter of a neighbour. In 1891 the store was damaged by fire. Castlegate presented a strange spectacle as cheeses, hams, tins of biscuits etc. were carried from the burning building. In 1821 the theatre behind the shop was open each night during race weeks for the 'nobility and the gentry'. This is now the Penrith Playhouse.

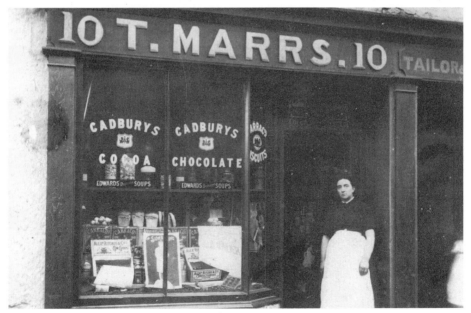

You can still see this shop-front in Penrith's Castlegate. Taken around 1905, it shows owner Mrs Mary Marrs, who ran the shop for forty years, selling sweets, chocolates and tobacco. She also baked bread, scones and teacakes. It is now the home of her granddaughter and husband. The property dates from the early eighteenth century.

A very early photograph of Castlegate. This decorated arch, stretching from the Museum Hotel to the house across the road, was almost certainly one of many erected to celebrate the occasion of the marriage of the Prince of Wales (later King Edward VII) to Princess Alexandra of Denmark at St George's Chapel, Windsor, on 10 March 1863. The house on the left with the family outside was at one time a public house, then a Temperance Hotel, and is now the Victoria Hotel. The first mention of the Victoria by name is in 1897; it was then the Victoria Temperance and Commercial and Family Hotel and the proprietor was John Pattinson.

The Simonini brothers standing in the doorway of their shop at No. 45 Castlegate around 1913. Adolpho (Simon) moved to Penrith from his home in Italy to work with his brother, Pietro, who had taken over Carlo Cardossi's ice-cream business in 1912. They also ran a successful fish and chip business. Later the family opened a shop in Little Dockray.

Railway carter Ted Ryelands with his decorated float carrying the Castletown Coronation May Queen of 1953, Pat Tomlinson, and her attendants, photographed in Castlegate beside the Royal Oak Inn which was run at that time by Pat's parents. The inn closed in 1962.

This former Westmorland County Council Fowler steam roller lay motionless at the Penrith foundry of Stalker Brothers in Castlegate for seven years before it was saved from the danger of being scrapped. It is seen here leaving the works after being bought by Amos and William Treloar, Haltwhistle, who planned to restore it. Mr George Stalker, who ran the business at that time (1969) is on the right, and his son Paul on the left. The Agricultural Engineering Firm of Stalker Bros, founded in 1851 by Jonathan Stalker, was the largest in the town. He had set up as a master blacksmith, making ploughs and other farm implements, but by the 1880s he was making and selling threshing-machines and carrying out repairs on steam engines. His two sons inherited the firm in 1889 and extended the property, becoming, as well as agricultural engineers, millwrights, boiler and implement makers, and iron and brass founders. The third Jonathan (1885–1969) adapted the firm to meet the changing needs of agriculture and witnessed the passing of the age of steam. His grandson Paul sold the foundry to the Penrith Steam Museum.

Penrith's other engineering works was G. & J. Thompson's of Brunswick Road. Pictured about 1920 are some of the workers and employers beside two of the Penrith Rural District Council's steam rollers in for repair. Penriths first steam roller was bought in 1895 and a shed constructed for it in old London Road.

A view from the Castle Park with Penrith Beacon in the background in 1963. Gone are Harry Pattinson's fruit and sweet shop on the right, and Tommy Johnstone's hardware shop on the left. The large warehouses built in 1872 along with the auction mart erected in 1881 behind the Agricultural Hotel were demolished in 1987. A supermarket now occupies the sight.

The Agricultural Hotel and Posting House, seen here at the turn of the century, was run by the Burns family for many years.

An unusual sight in Penrith in the 1950s was the visiting Bewcastle Hunt, with its members mounted on horseback and about to set out for a day's sport at Bowscar along with the pack of eager foxhounds. Normally, local hunts in the fell areas were followed on foot. The ruins of Penrith Castle can be seen in the background.

Penrith Castle. In the early part of this century the castle was owned by the London and North Western Railway Company. Inside the ruins the railway company had the stables for their horses. There was also a house there, as can be seen on the right of the photograph. Behind the castle Jos. Tremble & Sons had their nurseries, which were later taken over by Herd Bros, who had a shop in King Street. The castle was bought by the UDC in 1912. They partially restored it and opened up the surrounding grounds as the Castle Park in 1923.

Penrith Castle. As in the case of Brougham, it is not known who built the first fortress or castle in Penrith, but it is supposed to have been erected by Ralph Neville, the First Earl of Westmorland, to protect the inhabitants of 'Penreth' from Scottish invaders. The Duke of Gloucester, later to become Richard III (1483–5), is said to have repaired the castle. Richard Dudley, late steward of Penrith, had taken from the castle, by warrant of Anthony Barwise, thirty cartloads of stone to build a prison in Penrith. Different quantities were removed in the first year of King Edward VI's reign. It is not known who dismantled the castle.

Viewed from the railway bridge, workshops and warehouses in Cromwell Road, the wartime air-raid siren still on the roof, and Miss Rennie's house on the corner. The workshops and house, along with the home of Pat Coulston and his family, where work had already begun (as seen below), were demolished in 1957. The warehouses of G. & J. Graham were knocked down in 1986.

Castle Garage in Cromwell Road in the early 1930s. It was then owned by Frank Smith and petrol was 1s. 3d. a gallon. Having just been topped up with this costly fuel, the young man prepares to drive off in his Frazer Nash. Above the garage, Fidlers had a joiner's shop.

An early picture of the Castle Hotel in Castletown, the owner of that time, Mrs Robertshaw, at the door. The date is unknown but is before the First World War. The public house is still very busy today, being the only one in the suburb. In 1829 there were 57 public houses and 9 beer shops in Penrith. In former times people ate a lot of salted beef, mutton and bacon, which may have accounted for their inordinate thirst! The population of Penrith at that time was 5,383. By 1926 there were only 42 public houses.

A typical scene at the turn of the century: a coach and pair with its bowler-hatted driver trundles down the middle of King Street, with garages, hotels and shops on the right and J. Lawn's tobacconist's on the left. Until early in the nineteenth century, King Street was called Netherend, later Front Street, and came to an abrupt halt at its southern end. Later a large warehouse was demolished and the street was opened up via what is now Victoria Road. Further up the street lived a carrier, and his warehouse was the centre from which most of the local wagons set out for outlying towns and villages along dusty, rutted roads. The original Mitre Inn was built in 1669, and rebuilt in 1904 retaining its first door, which had lasted for 250 years. The inn was the birthplace of Trooper William Pearson, who survived the disastrous Charge of the Light Brigade, the cholera epidemic which preceded it, and also the severe Russian winter which followed. The Robin Hood Inn, despite ceasing to be an inn almost a century ago, has perhaps the most interesting history of all the hostelries, for it was here that William Wordsworth stayed with his friend, Raisley Calvert.

People throng King Street. The view is looking south from Market Square. A group of ladies chat in the street outside the *Advertiser* newspaper office, and a man with a hand-cart pauses to talk to a bowler-hatted acquaintance at Herd's corner.

A Christmas display at Mr Peter Grant's well-stocked shop in King Street. Tempting the customers is a lavish choice of geese, ducks, chickens, rabbits and game in abundance, as well as his usual stock of fish.

A row of laden grocer's carts stands outside Pears & Elliott's shop in King Street, ready for moving out into the villages surrounding Penrith with orders for goods. Orders had been taken previously by travellers calling on prospective customers.

Directly opposite Pears & Elliott's was the shop of the Wishart family, here shown with Mrs Wishart in the doorway. They sold hats, hosiery, ties, gloves and other items for the well-dressed man. The picture, from about 1900, obviously coincided with a drive to sell straw hats.

Armstrong and Fleming's King Street garage, *c.* 1920. Outside are two Rolls Royce cars. The one on the road belonged to the Shaw family of Rampsbeck, Ullswater. Standing beside the other car is the late Mr Jack Pounder, then a mechanic at the garage. Armstrong & Fleming were the local agents for Rolls Royce at that time. The *Herald* office now occupies the garage site.

Children stand outside the Crown Hotel as a coach prepares to leave. The hotel station van stands on the other side of the street.

The Crown Hotel decorated to celebrate the accession of King George V in 1910. This was one of the many posting houses that sprang up in the 1780s to cater for travellers using the mail coach service between Manchester and Glasgow. This was a costly way to travel 200 years ago; the rates for riding from Manchester to Penrith were 25s. inside and 15s. 6d. outside. This picture shows wagonettes and traps congregated to take tourists to various beauty spots in the district. The Siddle family's long link with the hotel ended in 1965. The Crown was demolished some years ago and a supermarket and offices now occupy the site.

The circus comes to town, *c.* 1890. After a parade through the town, elephants and their trainers turn into the cobbled Crown Square on their way to the Foundry Field where the big-top was usually erected.

Decorated arches were erected in Penrith to celebrate many royal occasions and to welcome royalty from England and Europe who frequently visited Lowther Castle. This one and another just visible in King Street were probably to welcome the Kaiser in 1895 or 1900.

A very popular and well-patronized drapers shop situated on the corner of King Street and Langton Street, around 1912, crammed with articles required by normal households such as blankets and bedding. The shop was run by Mr 'Totty' Lowis and his family.

Victoria Road earlier known as Dover Street, at the southern end of the town around 1904. Knight's fishing tackle shop was in existence for many years, and next to it was Bowerbank's Iron Foundry. The Salutation Hotel on the right is still there, and in 1920 Tinkler's built their garage further down the road. A farmer returns home in his horse and cart with his empty milk cans.

Pear Tree Yard is situated between Southend Road and Victoria Road. The yard is still there, but devoid of the old mansion and cottages: they were demolished in February 1925.

Brewery Yard was in Southend Road, opposite Pear Tree Yard. It was demolished in the 1950s. On the right of the picture can be seen the clinic.

Although only 8 ft wide at its narrowest point, many centuries ago Rowcliffe Lane or, earlier, Old Post Office Lane, was the principal street in the town. It was even used by pack horses in the days before stage coaches. Stage coaches first ran through Penrith for long journeys in 1763, and sedan chairs were used up to 1800. The tall many-windowed building was at one time the Black Lion Hotel, reputed to be one of the best inns in town, which later became Guests boot manufacturer and repair shop. It was originally the first post office. Next to the hotel was the Presbyterian manse, built in 1656 to serve the church housed in what is now Reeds Printing Works which was opened for worship in May 1785. The old manse later became a pawnshop run by Mr William Dean.

This nicely lit picture shows Alcock's tea mart and grocery premises on the left and Guests on the right. Moss Yard, at the lower end of the street, commemorates Peggy Moss, who owned a cake shop with bakery adjoining. By 1910 Rowcliffe Lane had lost its prestige and became one of the minor streets of the town. Ryan Yard, which also branched off from the lane, was so called because it belonged to the Ryan family for generations. The premises in it were known as Ryan's Lodging House. Accommodation was provided for countless wayfarers passing through or living in the town and for Irish navvies. It closed in December 1929 when the charge per night was 9d. It was used as a warehouse until the yard was demolished in 1961. In 1895 there were 3,660 people in lodging houses in the town, 2,839 adult males, 451 adult females, 79 males and 72 females between 8 and 21 years, and 123 males and 96 females under 8 years old.

Middlegate (the Long Front) was one of the main streets of old Penrith, and it is interesting to note that many yards, courts and passages led off from it. Some of these were inhabited by as many as a dozen families, who had their houses behind heavy wooden doors, bolted and barred against the raiding Scots. The north end was a cul-de-sac, with gardens stretching across the road, which was opened up on Jubilee Day, 1887. Behind a high wall was Musgrave Hall, the residence of Countess Ossalinsky, whose family sold Thirlmere to Manchester Corporation. The way northward, previously, was by way of Queen Street and over Fallowfield Bridge at the head of Brook Street. That was the way the rebel Scots entered Penrith in 1715 and 1745. In 1910 the brewery which stood on the right was pulled down to make room for the Alhambra Theatre and the shops which flanked it under a shopping arcade, all built by William Forrester. The Ship Hotel and Wilson Jespers building gave way to Burtons the tailors, in 1936. Milburns, cycle merchants, also had the motor agency for American Overland cars, built under licence in Lancashire around 1909.

A good view of the length of double pavement in Middlegate where, on market day, around 1919, smallholders and some farmers' wives seated themselves to display their ware. People came to buy butter, eggs and vegetables. Very prominent on the right of the picture is the high-class shop of Wilson Jespers, tailors and outfitters, next to the Ship Hotel.

Travelling along Middlegate on its way to the bus station in Sandgate is the Ribble bus bound for Patterdale. It has just passed the verandah, a glass-topped structure screening both shop-fronts and customers from rain and sun.

One of the last street traders in the town. Passers-by were attracted by the fresh produce that was offered for sale by Mr Harold Hardisty. There was no shortage of customers along Middlegate, where he took his stand in the 1950s.

Penrith Alhambra in Middlegate, built in 1910 by Mr William Forrester sen., was decorated for the Silver Jubilee of King George V and Queen Mary when this picture was taken in 1935. The Alhambra was not originally intended as a cinema, but as a public assembly hall, with a maple floor suitable for roller skating which was then very popular.

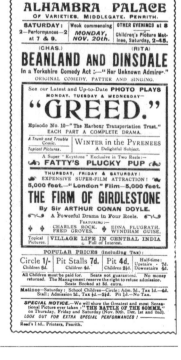

Handbills in different colours with a list of forthcoming attractions at the 'Alhambra Palace of Varieties' were delivered to households every week. This one must have been produced just after the First World War. A special notice says, 'we will be showing sensational pictures of the Battle of the Somme'.

Burrowgate in the 1920s, with the furniture showrooms and electrical department of Hetherington Bros on the left, and the Co-operative store on the way into Sandgate.

Penrith's first Co-operative Society shop was at the top of Castlegate and was established in 1890. It was vacated in 1901, moving into the new premises in Burrowgate. These premises later became Harry Pattinson's fruit and sweet shop, and in the small shop on the left, Willy Holmes, physically handicapped, carried on his shoe repair business for many years.

The new Co-op shop in Burrowgate in 1931, which was fitted out with a centralized cash tube system.

The General Manager of the Co-op makes a call in the village of Helton with his Trojan car. Country travellers faced all weathers. One of the Co-op employees, Mr Sisson, while travelling the Patterdale area, became snowbound and had to stay the night there. He reached Troutbeck station about five miles away the following morning by walking the wall tops and using wire fences as a guide.

Tomlinson's fish and chip shop in Burrow-gate around 1930.

Mrs Thompson stands in the doorway of her small shop at the foot of Sandgate. This building was demolished in 1935 to make way for Thos Altham's large store.

Farmers' wives in town with their large baskets of produce. This was the 'butter and egg' market in Sandgate, *c.* 1914.

All the houses at the foot of Sandgate leading into Albert Street, including Sharp Bros' painting and plumbing business, were demolished in the early 1950s to make way for the new Ribble bus station.

Further up Sandgate from the cottages in the previous photograph was this charming early Georgian house built in 1718. The little girl stands in the entrance to Douglas Yard (note the brass 'toe nebs' on her clogs, shining), *c.* 1905. The house was demolished many years ago. Above it can be seen three cottages. Before conversion this was Sandgate Hall, built in 1640 by the Fletchers of Hutton and later passed into the hands of the Grave family. Builder William Grisenthwaite lived in the Hall for about twelve years and in about 1860 decided to convert his old home into three cottages and built more cottages in the grounds. These have now been incorporated into a new building project with the old cottages restored and new ones added.

At the head of Sandgate is Crozier Lodge. In 1865 this mansion was a girls' school; some of the pupils look out of a window while two teachers chat to the top-hatted gardener. Miss Brewis was the headmistress.

Corner shop memories. This little corner shop on Meeting House Lane, run by Mrs Jessie Campbell for three years, was demolished along with the adjoining cottages in April 1958.

A hundred yards further on, at the top of Hunter Lane, was Mr Ernest Dawson's grocers shop. In this picture taken in the 1930s we see hams and sausages dangling from the ceiling and a large and colourful array of biscuit tins; fragrant smells greeted customers, especially on 'weighing up' days. Mr Dawson and his son David are behind the counter. The shop is now Hunter Lane post office.

At the lower end of Hunter Lane by the turning into Queen Street was the cycle and repair shop of Mr Joseph Campbell and his partner Mr Bowe, who sold Fleet Bicycles with the World's Worthiest Wheel. In an advertisement in the *Penrith Observer* of 12 August 1902 they were the sole agents for Unity Cycles, and in their workshop 'free wheels [were] fitted on the shortest notice'. About two centuries ago this was a farm, as can be observed by the shop frontage, which at one period was farmed by a Mr Relph. It is now a television repair shop.

The attractive and well-kept business premises of Purdie, Water and Gas Fitter, Painters and Decorators, in Queen Street were about to be transferred to Great Dockray when this photograph was taken.

One part of the town that suffered during heavy rain was Queen Street. The main culprit for this flooding was the 'Thacka Beck', which flows under the town.

Wilson Row in the early 1950s, prior to the row of older cottages, built in 1690, being demolished in 1969.

Demolition begins on the old houses at the junction of Wilson Row and Duke Street. On the right of the picture is the Congregational church, built on the site of the old Ebenezer chapel in 1865 at a cost of £3,500. It closed in 1991 and was converted into eleven flats. It is now known as Church Mews.

Friar Street in the 1930s. Through the archway was Factory Yard, later known as Friar's Buildings. As well as the thriving weaving industry, of around 1800, many other activities were carried on here. There was a bakehouse kept for many years by Mr and Mrs W. Boak. People of the area used to prepare their own bread and take it to the large oven fired with coke from the nearby gasworks. 'Tatie Pots' were heated, and food was also prepared for hotels and shops. The yard also had links with education and religion. There was a School of Industry, where needlework and other skills were taught to about fifty poor girls. 'Penny readings' were available to the many people who could neither read nor write in those days, and later on an Evangelical Mission was run by Mr John Robson. Elsewhere in the yard were a number of old tenement houses. The old yard and all the other old buildings seen in the picture were demolished in the 1960s.

William Thompson took over the White Horse, Friar Street in 1869. The last tenants, until it closed in 1973, were Mr and Mrs Stanley Mann. A century ago it was the headquarters of Penrith Cricket Club and Friars Bowling Club. In early 1984 the White Horse and shop were demolished, and the last vestige of the Old Friar Street as a residential area disappeared. It is thought that John Thompson the artist painted the sign.

Friar Street on a wet day in 1959. During periods of heavy rain Friar Street and the surrounding area were prone to flooding. All the buildings in the picture have now gone, except for Mostyn Hall and the old Friarage at the far end on the right.

The Regent Cinema opened on 2 December 1933 with the film *Cavalcade* and closed its doors for the last time on 1 March 1984 with the film *Baby Love*. The cinema enjoyed its moment of greatest glory in 1980, when Princess Alexandra visited for the première of *My Brilliant Career*. The Regent is now a furniture store.

The Exchange Hotel, Angel Lane became a temperance hostelry for farmers attending Penrith market in 1878. It had been rebuilt as a place of entertainment which could house 700 people and had stabling for 70 horses. In 1909 the proprietor was T. Thistlewaite, who offered board and lodgings at 22s. 6d. per week, but for most of the twentieth century it was the business premises of Howes, the drapers. Known as Silver Street until 1829, Angel Lane, in which the Exchange was situated, was a narrow thoroughfare filled with flourishing shops and probably named from the Angel Inn which stood at the Dockray end. The Fleece Inn was at the other end.

Princess Street leads from Great Dockray to Crown Square. All the buildings on the left were demolished after the Second World War, including the Wool Mart. The houses on the right remain, except for the shop on the far right of the picture, at that time occupied by Mr and Mrs Allison. Entry to the Two Lions, at one time Gerard Lowther's house, was through the narrow alleyway between the buildings. In Princess Street around 1875 was Jenny Dalton's Dame School for young children, and many of the older generation received their early training at this little establishment. Centuries ago Princess Street, like Rowcliffe Lane, was an important artery for the pack-horse traders of the town, before King Street came to be the principal thoroughfare.

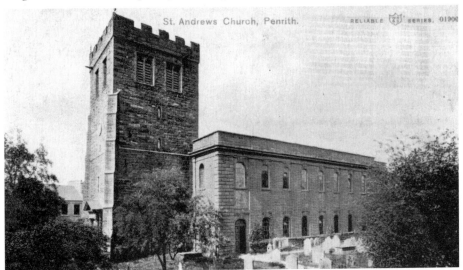

St Andrew's church was built, with the exception of the tower, towards the end of 1720 though the foundation stone was actually laid on 10 April 1721. In February 1723, after the building had been completed for several months, it was formally opened and consecrated by Dr William Nicolson, Bishop of Derry and previously rector of Great Salkeld.

The Giant's Grave stands on the north side of the parish church. The grave consists of four hog-back stones and two stone pillars each about 10 ft high. There are many conflicting stories as to who is actually buried here, if anyone at all. Popular legend says the stones mark the grave of Owen Caesarius, King of Cumbria from 920 to 937, but the crosses and connecting stones are probably separate memorials dating from different parts of the tenth century. On the right of the picture can be seen the old Grammar School.

Scholars and their masters outside the old Queen Elizabeth Grammar School in St Andrew's churchyard in 1907. The school was erected in 1567. The new school on Skirsgill Road took its place in 1915.

Also in the churchyard is the Tudor House, a picturesque building bearing the letters and date RB1563, a perfect specimen of the architecture of the Tudor period. It is believed to have been the home of Roger Bertram, although there is no reference to him in any old records. This is understood to be the oldest house in the town, at any rate the oldest with a date. It is now part of the Tudor Café.

Beacon Lodge, situated at the entrance to the Beacon, was built in 1818 and was the Forresters' residence. It is now known as Caroline Cottage.

The Beacon Pike, at 937 ft above sea level, was erected in 1719. Constructed of red sandstone, it commands a splendid view of the mountain scenery of Cumbria. Beacon Hill is a popular walk for local people and visitors alike. The last time the Beacon fire was lit was in 1745, when the Highlanders were retreating through Westmorland. A number of years ago the top of the Pike was damaged by lightning, as can be seen in the photograph. The property is owned by the Earl of Lonsdale.

SECTION THREE

Castles, Halls and other Buildings

Lowther Castle.

This picture shows the long queue waiting to look through the home of the Lowthers before it was eventually gutted. Apart from the large staff employed in the castle, very few ordinary people had ever ventured inside. The empty shell is now all that remains.

Lord and Lady Lonsdale on their Golden Wedding Anniversary, 27 June 1928.

Lord Lonsdale, Commanding Officer of the Westmorland and Cumberland Yeomanry.

The drawing room at Lowther Castle. In its heyday Lowther Castle was a splendid palace situated in a park of some 1,000 acres and styled 'the Windsor of the North'. It was furnished in a style of great opulence and had picture and sculpture galleries and antiquarian treasures from all parts of the world. The Lowther family has lived in Westmorland from time immemorial, and is one of the oldest in the country. Perhaps their origin was Danish, for a Danish settlement existed at Lowther, as three Viking hog-back tombstones in Lowther churchyard testify. The castle had its origin in an old medieval manor house, which was extended in the seventeenth century by Sir John Lowther and his sons. In the early part of the eighteenth century, during the life of Henry, the third Viscount Lonsdale, a great deal of Lowther Hall was burnt down. It remained a partial ruin for seventy years, until James, the First Earl of Lonsdale, began rebuilding the house to the 'castle' design of Sir Robert Smirke. Unfortunately, James never saw it completed as he died in 1802, and his successor, a distant cousin, who was recreated First Earl of Lonsdale, finished the castle during his lifetime. Many royals stayed there over the years, including Queen Victoria when she was a child. The 1940s saw great changes at Lowther Castle. In April 1944 Hugh Cecil Lowther, Fifth Earl of Lonsdale, died at the age of 87. His wife Grace had died three years previously, in May 1941, aged 86. Both are buried in the churchyard, overlooking the river, and not in the family mausoleum at Lowther, both graves being marked with simple crosses of granite. Because of the heavy death duties the castle was closed in 1947, and in a sale running for several weeks the contents and fabric were sold. Lord Lonsdale, also known as the 'Yellow Earl', will be remembered for as long as boxing continues as the originator of the system of Lonsdale Belts, which he set up in 1909. He was also famous for his car collection. Up to the First World War he owned at least fourteen private cars, mostly Napiers.

Brougham Castle stands on the south bank of the River Eamont. Its site has been of strategic importance since the first century AD, when Agricola and the Roman armies crossed the Eamont on their way to Scotland. The first historical mention was in 1234. In the Middle Ages Brougham marked the north-western limit of a great tract of land, stretching from the River Eamont to Stainmore. The last notable occupant of the castle was Lady Anne Clifford (1590–1676), a lady of strong character, determined benevolence and active devotion to family tradition, who ruled the Clifford estates for many years in the style of her medieval forebears. Brougham Castle was one of the great residences of the north and centuries ago English and Scottish kings visited there. Lady Anne's successors, the Earls of Thanet, neglected the castle, and in 1714 it was finally stripped of its lead and timber, and left to decay. In 1928 the castle was placed in the guardianship of the State.

Greystoke Castle was rebuilt in the late seventeenth century at great expense, after a disastrous fire in the time of Charles I, by Charles Henry Howard. On 4 May 1868 a second fire again destroyed not only most of the building but many treasures and family portraits. All that was left was a massive tower and vaulted cellar, but on these foundations Henry Howard built a beautiful and delightful habitation standing in a park of 6,000 acres, through which no public road or footpath passes. When Stafford Howard, a former High Sheriff of Cumberland, died in 1991 the castle had been in possession of the family for over 400 years.

Dacre Castle was built in 925 and it is probably the oldest castle in the north. Early in the tenth century three kings met at Dacre Castle, which is three miles from Penrith: they were Athelstan, first King of England, Constantine, King of Scotland and Eugenius, King of Cumbria.

Brougham Hall stands in a charming situation on the right bank of the River Lowther. In its day it was a lovely castellated edifice and was originally fortified, having had a long and colourful history. It was purchased in 1727 by the Broughams from its early owners for £3,000, to become the proud ancestral mansion of that family, the most notable member of which was Lord Chancellor Brougham, who was called to the English Bar in 1808, which meant that he became the first Baron Brougham and Vaux. The fourth Lord Brougham and Vaux had a flamboyant life style, and although he twice 'broke the bank' at Monte Carlo he lost everything and by 1932 was forced to sell some of the Hall's antique furniture to cover his debts. In 1934 his marriage ended in divorce, and a few months later Brougham Hall was sold to Major Carleton Cowper, who subsequently began to demolish it. A year later, following the outbreak of war in 1939, the army made use of the Hall.

The Library, Brougham.

Lord and Lady Brougham on the lawn at Brougham Hall in the early thirties. The fourth Lord Brougham and Vaux married Valerie French, the daughter of a First World War Commander, in 1931. It was an extravagant occasion, with a hundred tenants of the estate and staff of the Hall present at St Margaret's church, Westminster. A ball was held in Penrith, with lavish presents for all who attended. Unfortunately, this marriage was later dissolved.

Brougham Hall knocker. This splendid bronze door-knocker, a replica of the Durham Cathedral Sanctuary knocker, disappeared during the war, its destination unknown.

The sale of stone and timber during the demolition.

Edenhall mansion, built in the Italian style and comprising 37½ acres, was erected in 1821 to become the residence of Sir George and Lady Musgrave. It was razed to the ground in 1934 when the land on which it stood was purchased by Major Mead. The hall itself was sold for demolition and everything came under the hammer: doors, windows, oak panelling, fire grates – even a white marbled mantelpiece with the Musgrave arms emblazoned on it was sold for eleven shillings. The remaining shell of the mansion was sold to Mr Irving, a Carlisle contractor, for £500.

The demolition of Edenhall mansion, which began immediately after the sale.

Hutton-in-the-Forest. The present mansion is a noble structure created around an original pele tower by Sir George Fletcher in the reign of Charles II, the architect being the famous Inigo Jones. The first holders of the Manor of Hutton were obliged to do curtain services for the king, maintaining some of his forests and holding his stirrup when he mounted his horse at Carlisle. The manor was sold by Thomas Hutton in 1605 to Sir Richard Fletcher and then passed by the marriage of the heiress to the family of Vane of whom the present Lord Inglewood is a descendant.

Catterlen Hall, built in 1577, is now converted into a farmhouse and was in the possession of the Saxon Haldane in the reign of William the Conqueror. Over the door of the kitchen is the dripstone, bearing the arms of Vaux, with a legend: 'Let mercy and faithfullness never go from thee.' Underneath it says, 'At this time is Roland Vaux Lord of this place and builded this house in the year of God 1577.'

Yanwath Hall is a fourteenth–century fortified manor house which was at one time owned by the Lowthers. The old Roman road crossed the River Eamont at Yanwath and the old tower at the Hall was erected to guard the ford. The river divides Cumberland and Westmorland.

The old nunnery near Kirkoswald, six miles from Penrith, was a popular beauty spot visited by tourists because of its setting by the River Eden with attractive woodland walks and waterfalls. Coaches from the George and Crown Hotels ran excursions to this spot

Two eighteenth-century houses alike in every detail and known jointly as Wordsworth House were erected by Isaac Parker and William Wilson in 1792. The one on the left was occupied at one time by a Dr Livingstone and the other by William Wordsworth's cousin John, who died in 1819. Penrith Urban Council bought the houses in 1904 to convert into a Town Hall. A great controversy arose which became of national interest when it was claimed that the houses were in good classical style and probably from the design of Robert Adam, and that it would be a desecration to alter the front in any way. With the support of Canon Rawnsley, the council agreed to retain the staircase and original doors and windows. The conversion work which had temporarily ceased was resumed in March 1905. There was a more encouraging response to these objectionable alterations from the other side of the Atlantic! From East 91st Street, New York, came a letter expressing interest in and support for the free library part of the new development. Millionaire Mr Andrew Carnegie sent £1,200 to help Penrith to 'provide library accommodation of a superior character'.

The conversion of Wordsworth House into the Town Hall cost around £7,000 in 1905. Stopping for a few minutes to pose for the cameraman are the thirty-five stonemasons and carpenters, etc. who were involved in the work.

The completed Town Hall, *c.* 1910. The town's library and museum were situated in the rear of the building.

Scaws Farmhouse. Situated above the town, the building dates from the beginning of the last century. The front was ornamented in the castellated style so that it would be clearly seen from Lowther Castle.

SECTION FOUR
Villages

Excursions to Ullswater. During the summertime in the early 1900s many popular railway excursions came from the Lancashire cotton towns to Penrith station, where they were met by wagonettes drawn by two, three or four horses or even by the modern charabancs like the Mosley owned by Siddles of the Crown Hotel. These day trippers then enjoyed the magnificent lakeland scenery by going either to Pooley Bridge, then to Glenridding and back on the lake steamer, or up to the summit of Kirkstone Pass and down again, which was quite a hazardous and exciting journey.

A walk to Eamont Bridge and a stroll by the river was a popular Sunday afternoon walk in summer for many Penrithians. The bridge over the River Eamont, which divides Cumberland and Westmorland, was built around 1425 on the site of an older bridge.

An Eamont Bridge farmer is returning home from his milk round in Penrith and has paused at the Toll Bar at the top of Kemplay, *c.* 1904. It will be a hazardous descent down the steep gradient to the village because of the snow. There remain today four toll bar cottages on the outskirts of the town, at Brougham, Skirsgill, Newton Road and at Kemplay. In 1880 tolls were levied on farm produce and animals entering the town, from one penny for a basket of butter or eggs to two pence for a cow and four pence for a horse.

Mr Harry Savage has paused to give his hard-working horses a brief rest. Both are sweating profusely, hauling heavy timber on their cart to Sarginson's sawmill in Eamont Bridge, *c.* 1920.

Harry and Sarah Savage lived at Low Mill, beside the river. Mrs Savage and her grandson Geoff have been scattering corn for the hens.

The Welcome Inn at Eamont Bridge, sometimes known as the Salutation was clearly still in operation in 1904. Horse-mounted travellers head up Kemplay Bank towards town, while two lady cyclists choose to walk down the steep gradient rather than risk brake failure. Note the very high wall on the left of the road; this was lowered in 1948. A large oil painting depicting an Englishman clasping hands with a kilted Scotsman was fixed on the gable end below the signboard; it has been suggested that this was the work of John Thompson, Penrith artist and hairdresser of Angel Lane. Towards the end of 1913 the inn, then owned by Glasson's, was closed, so after over a century it ceased to welcome visitors to Cumberland.

Kirkby Thore at the beginning of the century was a quiet, peaceful village, especially compared to the busy place it is today, with a large volume of heavy traffic connected with the Gypsum Works. It has a pleasant situation near the confluence of the Eden and Troutbeck and much of it was built out of the ruins of Whelph Castle. The children are standing by the post office of earlier days.

A large crowd with big umbrellas has assembled on the green at Temple Sowerby on a wet day in 1884 to witness the raising of the 50 ft maypole in preparation for May Day. The masonry work around the base was carried out by Mr John Parker of Cliburn to the design of Mr Furness of Temple Sowerby.

The May Queen of Temple Sowerby for 1924 was Elsie Sisson, seen here on Daisy, who was owned by local farmer Mr Thomas Goulding of West View Farm. Daisy was bought at Carlisle Auction just before the First World War and died during the Second World War.

On a finer May Day in Temple Sowerby in 1924 children dance around a much smaller maypole.

Children of Great Salkeld celebrate Empire Day in 1909 by dancing round the maypole.

The Shepherds Inn situated in the centre of the picturesque village of Langwathby on the banks of the River Eden. The stone bridge carrying the road was swept away in the early morning of 25 March 1968 by flood water driven by high winds.

The catastrophic aftermath of the sweeping away of Langwathby bridge.

Goose pluckers at Low Farm, Langwathby, Christmastime 1904.

Langwathby, *c.* 1953. The May Queen and her attendants on their decorated horse-drawn cart lead the procession past the Shepherds Inn and the war memorial.

The importance of farming in the area is evident from the famous Lazonby Auction Mart, built near the station around 1910. With its weekly Wednesday auctions and the famous autumn sheep sales, it is now renowned as the biggest in the north of England. The photograph is from around 1914.

The family at Blencarn Hall enjoy the sunshine in the farmyard in 1907.

The village shop in Blencarn in 1907, with the proprietor John McDonald and his wife in the garden.

East fellside farmers and their wives help each other out at the annual clipping and branding of their large flocks of sheep.

Skirwith, one of several villages open to the ravages of the Helm Wind, a wind of unknown origin common only along the east fellside of the Pennines. Because it blows so strongly, a local saying in Cumberland dialect is, 'It's fit t'blo' t' nebs off t' geuse!' ('It's fit to blow the beaks off the geese!'). Along the topside of the village is the post office and store and the drapers and grocers shop of Lydia Studholme.

A few of the local inhabitants of the east fellside village of Renwick pose for the camera in 1908 as a car rumbles through in the early days of motoring.

Farmer John Robinson of Gate Ghyll Farm, Threlkeld, completes the last stitch of the day with his team of horses, Jewel and Fanny, in the shadow of Blencathra in 1958.

The Mitchinson family outside their home at Mellfell View, Troutbeck, where they also ran a small shop in 1907. Village postman Jack Airey lived next door. The two cottages were situated between the railway and the beck. The branch line from Penrith to Keswick was closed on 4 March 1972.

After calling a halt at the Kirkstone Inn for refreshments and to admire the view, passengers make ready to descend the steep and tortuous pass. Pity the poor cameraman: he had to cycle to the top – no fifteen-speed gears in those days!

Coming down a steep section of the pass, the leading two horses in perfect step and picking their way over the uneven road surface. The last three wagonettes are in a cloud of dust.

MY *Raven* leaving Glenridding for Pooley Bridge and calling at Howtown. *Raven* was launched on Ullswater in 1889 by Miss Parkin of Howtown having cost £2,650. Kaiser William II sailed in her during his visit to Lowther Castle in 1900. Only three steamers ever plied the lake; first was *The Enterprise*, a paddle steamer launched in 1859, then *The Lady of the Lake*, launched in 1877. *The Lady* was damaged by fire in 1965.

The winter of 1946/7. Aira Force, the famous 80 ft waterfall immortalized by Wordsworth, is seen here in winter garb having come to a standstill as the beck froze.

SECTION FIVE

Work and School

This method of taking home the hay to the stackyard would have been regarded as very modern in 1912. The horse has been replaced by an ingenious converted car, and all the family has come out to help and watch.

Fair Hill. A cattle fair was often held on the outskirts of the town, at the place known as Fair Hill. The White Ox public house stands on the left. The area behind is now a housing estate and beyond is the golf course. In the late 1700s this was the Penrith Racecourse, and records of meetings date back to 1765. The most memorable event of its kind ever held there was the great review of the Cumberland and Westmorland Volunteers in 1867. The last race meeting took place in 1896 as part of Queen Victoria's Diamond Jubilee celebrations. Regular race meetings had ceased ten years previously.

Sale day for cattle in the top ring at Penrith Auction Mart just after the Second World War. An interesting prosecution before Penrith magistrates in November 1883 was of Thomas Sisson, an auctioneer employed by Penrith Farmer Auction Co., who was summoned by the Board of Health that he, 'not being a licensed hawker', had sold eight sheep at the mart without paying toll. The magistrates imposed a fine of one shilling, without costs.

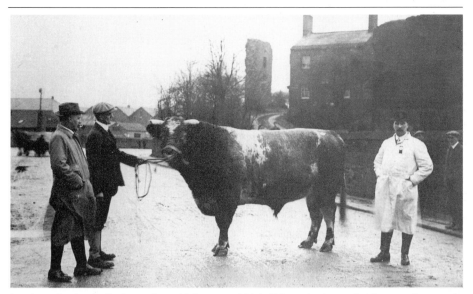

A prize-winning bull pictured on 10 January 1911. Prize-winning animals were frequently taken from the nearby auction to be photographed in front of the old castle. Holding the bull is its owner, Mr Tom Lowthian of Winderhall. It is not known who the other two gentlemen are.

An amicable discussion between Inspector Brown of the RSPCA and Dick Turner, for many years Foreman at the town's busy Auction Mart. He and his family lived in a small house inside the mart, moving there in 1913. After twenty-five years they moved out to live in Castlegate and in 1954 Dick retired from the company after forty-two years. Auction and cottage were demolished in 1987.

Blacksmith Mr Riley shoeing a horse in his shop at Milton Street in 1927, while Mr John Bowman sen. of Cockell View and his son look on.

Seen here with his horse and cart is Joseph Bulman, one of the many carriers working from different collection points in the town, usually hotels. Mr Bulman was one of forty-nine carriers, three of them women, who carried goods to all the villages and outlying areas. In the early part of the century he operated from the Mitre Hotel in King Steet, leaving around 2.30 on Tuesdays for Newby by Cliburn and Morland.

The Station Hotel at Blencow is now known as Clickham Inn. In the 1920s James Dalton of No. 13 Castlegate, Penrith, was employed as a carter for Glassons Breweries; he is seen here delivering beer to the public house.

Eight carters of the LMS Railway Company in 1948 stabling their horses after a hard day's work delivering goods around the town. They are, left to right: Billy Coulthard, Billy Stewart, Jack Stout, Ted Hodgson, Jimmy Edgar, Bobby Nicholson, Tony Atkinson and Herbert Stout. Each carter would carry up to four loads a day around the town.

Scaws Estate, 1949. Work goes ahead on Penrith's biggest post-war housing scheme. The builder was local man, Mr Robert (Bob) Reay, who won the first contract for eighty houses. The number of houses eventually built was about 200. Bulldozer driver Ernie Douglas levels the land on Brentfield Way for the next block of council houses, a large number of which are of an unusual design, being red sandstone fronted, with sandstone pillars and dormer windows. Costing £1,150 to build at the time, they are now among the most desirable dwellings in Penrith in terms of character, design and situation.

Penrith head post office and Conservative Club in Crown Square, decorated for the Silver Jubilee of King George V and Queen Mary in 1935. The old post office was approximately 100 years old when demolished in 1962; the new one, with a much larger sorting office, opened on 7 December 1964.

Inside the old sorting office just after the Second World War.

Last 'Mail Click' pick up at Penrith. History was made on Friday evening on 1 October 1971, when the pouches of mail were snatched from the line-side apparatus by the London-bound 'up special' travelling post office, watched by a crowd of sightseers. The Penrith apparatus was the last in use in the country. The system was introduced in 1838 and there were 240 collection points throughout Britain. Left: postmen Reg Savage and Ron Bamber hang up the heavy leather pouches. Right: the TPO flashes past with the open net only a few yards away.

The 'Up' North Western TPO, hauled by the rebuilt 'Scot' *The Lancashire Regiment* approaching the line-side apparatus at Townhead at around 9.30 on a summer's night in the early 1950s.

This picture shows the immense difficulty that local postmen had in delivering the mail during the severe winter of 1936/7. The small Morris van has just room to squeeze through between the high banks of snow.

The Penrith to Martindale postbus, the first in England, which began on 30 October 1967, seen here passing Winter Crag Farm in the winter of 1969/70. Photographed by the author who was one of the first drivers.

Blencowe Grammar School. Pupils and teachers photographed beside the old school, c. 1865. Built in 1577 and rebuilt in 1795 at a cost of £358 4s. 3d. the school was founded by Thomas Burbank, a native of Blencowe. The headmaster in 1892 was Thomas Fawcett BA, a local man.

Teachers and pupils at Blencowe Primary School, *c.* 1910.

Robinson's School in Middlegate was built in 1670, probably by subscription, but a Mr William Robinson of London, who was a native of Penrith, had ten years prior to this bequested the sum of £20 per annum for ever to be payable out of his premises in Grub Street, London, for the bringing up and educating of poor girls. Several other bequests were afterwards made. A spinning and knitting school was also carried on in the upper room of the building. The school closed many years ago and is now the home of Penrith Museum; an extension built on the end is the Tourist Information Centre. Over the doorway is the inscription EX: SUMTIBUS: DN WILL: ROBINSON. CIVIS. LOND. ANNO 1670.

A group of infants in the playground of Robinson's School in 1905. Their headmistress, Miss Simpson, is on the left of the picture.

Benson Row, *c.* 1940. The Boys' National School, built in 1874 on ground given by the Earl of Lonsdale and partly hidden by the large tree, was demolished in the 1980s. The tree was felled many years ago. On the right in the wall can be seen the old watering trough for cattle and horses known as Hutton Spout. It was fed by a spring in the Flatt Field. The spout was provided by a member of the Hutton family around 1735. It still exists, but without the water.

A.B. Sinclair, headmaster of the Boys' National School, supervises the digging up of the school playing field to grow vegetables during the First World War.

The pupils of Brunswick Road Girls' School in 1938 or '39.

People and Leisure

Cycling was all the rage at the turn of the century. Mrs Wishart and her friends pose here for their photographs in Skirsgill Lane. Arnison's Drapers had the sole right to supply in the area the 'Rideasy' improved cycling and walking skirts. Thos Altham and Son sold New Hudson cycles for ladies, while Joseph Bowerbank made some models in his own workshop.

Factory Yard was once the centre of Penrith's weaving industry. Mr James Sisson of Foster Street was the last of the Penrith weavers, working from 1846 to 1908, latterly in his weaving shop in Graham Street. Interviewed by the *Herald* in 1908, he recalled that there were many looms in Factory Yard, but even more in Foster Street, with at least twenty working looms in four different weaving sheds. It is interesting to recall that James married an Irish girl, Margaret Loney, at Gretna Green in July 1853. James Sisson was the author's great uncle.

Kaiser's Visit. With bunting and flags flying, town councillors dressed in their Sunday best await the arrival of the Kaiser at Penrith railway station on 14 August 1895, on his first visit to Lowther Castle. He stayed there for five days. Left to right: G. Wainwright, T. Thistlewaite, J. Fleming, B. Sweeten, C. Farrer, R. Slack, J. Scott, H.S. Inglewood, Dr Joseph Altham, H. Winter, R.B. Neville.

This group of people, about sixty in all, is the entire Hetherington family and their workforce, photographed in 1900 in front of No. 2 Brunswick Square, at that time the home of Tom (seated in the centre with arms folded). He was the eldest of the three brothers who all ran several successful businesses in the town until about 1931. The other two were Dick and Alf. It is not known what this festive occasion was, but the gathering are dressed in their smartest clothes and most of the men are wearing buttonholes.

The marriage of Miss Sarah Robson to Mr William Harrison in 1897. Taken outside the bride's home at Johnstone Farm, Johnby, the photograph is notable for the beautiful dresses and fashionable hats of the guests.

The village wedding of Mr Charles Bell and Miss Martha Fisher at St Cuthbert's church, Great Salkeld, in August 1916.

Penrith's first fire-engine, a 'Merryweather', was purchased in June 1893 at a cost of £320. The local board also splashed out on new uniforms for the firemen, the tunics costing £1 9s. each and the helmets 17s. 6d. They are seen here outside the public offices in Friargate.

Penrith and District Fire Brigade and their engine in front of the Town Hall in 1919. The fire brigade was formed in 1893 and provided with a steam engine and ¾ mile of hose.

Lord Baden-Powell inspects Penrith's Boy Scouts in front of the Town Hall. The exact date is not known but it is probably about 1920.

The Penrith Town Band photographed in 1964 outside their headquarters at that time, the Mitre Inn in King Street, with their leader Ken Braithwaite and, behind him, mine host Mr George Cranswick. The band was founded on 7 April 1894, when it was known as the Penrith Sons of Temperance Band.

A major change occurred in 1943 when, after much discussion, it was decided that the band should become The National Fire Service A Division Band for the duration of the war. The band was photographed in NFS uniform in 1944 outside Hutton Hall in Friar Street with bandmaster and conductor Charlie Wannop sen. In 1946 the name changed to the British Legion Band and in 1962 was changed again, this time to the Penrith Town Band.

Wartime members of the Penrith National Fire Service outside their headquarters at Hutton Hall in Friargate. Back row, left to right: George Armer, Edwin Thompson, John Flint, Jack Crone, Wilf Pickering, Roland Hill, George Reay, Cliff Sisson, George Stalker, William Reed, Jack Crew and Ernie Ireland. The ladies are Peggy Cook, Nancy Currah and Edna Marsden. Front row: John Stewart, Harold Birbeck, Tom Nicholson, Joe Scott, Ronnie Wilkinson, Tom Varty, Dennis Turner, Les Watson and Ronnie Pears.

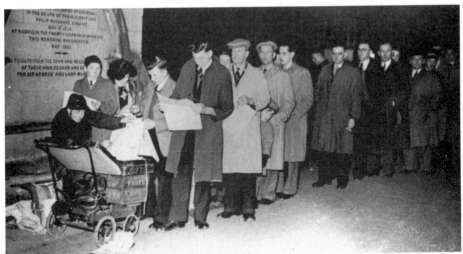

An enthusiastic crowd of football fans queue on Saturday night to buy the evening sports paper from Tommy Borrowdale, one of Penrith's well known 'characters', disabled but anxious to make a living. The occasion was the Penrith club's long run in the Amateur Cup in 1946/7, running out eventual winners 3–2 at Darlington after playing five matches with West Auckland. They beat Crook 3–0 in the next round. But, alas, the big one at Wembley was not to be, as they lost 5–3 to Willington, another Northern League team, in the next round.

The inauguration of Penrith's new ambulance in 1949. Town councillors and other officials present were, left to right: Mr Wharton of Eamont Bridge, Cdr. Jackson, Mr Mawson, Mr Tatters of Hornby Hall, Capt. Hill, Col. Lowther, Mr Huntley, Freddie Bell and Mr V. Yeates.

ATC Pioneers of 1942. Sixty-eight cadets of the Penrith 1247 Squadron of the Air Training Corps photographed in July 1942, with their instructors and commanding officer Flight Lieutenant J.H. Ellam (centre front), the squadron's greatest achievement in almost fifty years came in June 1988 with the award of the prestigious Lees trophy. The trophy, given to the squadron judged best in the United Kingdom, was presented by Air Commodore P.G. Naz.

Who can identify the five ladies in this mystery picture? The glass negative was found in a dustbin in Southend Road many years ago and it would be interesting to know who these charming people were, attired so smartly, and what the occasion.

Castletown Thursday soccer team in the 1903/4 season. The side played on a pitch at Newton Gate, just outside the town. All the people on the photograph were Castletonians, except the centre half Isaac Turner and club official Billy Howson, although they married Castletown girls! The team pictured are Ernest Stewart, Bill Pearson, Charlie Varty, Herbert Thompson, Isaac Turner, ? Ellwood, Jack Sisson, Arthur Carruthers, Joe Nicholson, Stanley Wilson, and Ben Sweeten. The officials are Fred Wilson, Tommy Johnstone, Billy Howson, T. Pearson and ? Huntingdon.

This pre-First World War picture is of the Penrith Butchers football team, winners of the Penrith & District Medals. The P&D League was started in the 1890s and carried on for over sixty years. The Cup Final was held every Easter Monday on the Penrith ground and always attracted over a thousand spectators.

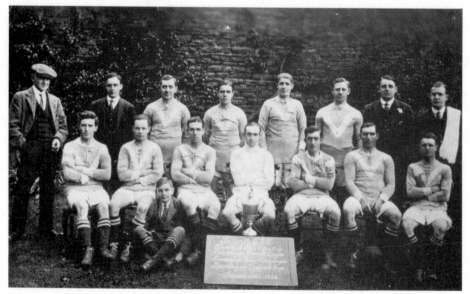

Penrith AFC with their trainers. In the 1921/2 season they were winners of the Eden Valley Cup, Penrith & District League, Penrith and District Cup and were runners-up in the Eden Valley League.

Eight members of the Friars Bowling Club with trophies won in 1933.

Bert Stanaway bowls the first wood at the start of a new season at the Castle Park Bowling Club in the early 1950s while the rest of the enthusiastic members look on.

Ian Brocklebank proudly receives his trophy from the Gala Queen after winning the 100 yd sprint at the 1956 Penrith Gala.

A group of young men out for a stroll on Sunday afternoon photographed beside the River Eamont at Pokey Dubs. About two miles out of town, this was one of many popular walks for Penrithians.

Only three to go. The Elliott family, enjoying a game of putting in the Castle Park in 1928, arrive at the 16th.

Penrith Swimming Club's stretch of the River Eamont at Frenchfield was a busy place at the height of the summer. Founded in 1881 by Alderman J. Simpson Yeates, it was originally for men only; when women were eventually admitted special times were reserved for them. The club went from strength to strength, attaining a record membership of 1,140 in 1933.

A group of hardy Penrith swimmers photographed at Frenchfield in November 1939. Back row, left to right: Alan Chapelhow, Les Sisson, Bruce Lewis. Front row: Walter Hall, Margaret Lewis, Jack Stoddart, William Brown (secretary), Arthur Chapelhow, Sheila Tinkler and Roland Kirkbride.

Beside the old snuff mill in Skirsgill Lane was a shallow pool in the River Eamont that was popular with local children. On 16 January 1937 the century-old mill closed. For many years it was owned by the Nevison family before being sold to a Kendal firm.

Skating on Edenhall Pond was a popular sport in winter. The enthusiasts continued until after sunset, the pond being lit by car headlamps.

The Penrith Melody Makers Dance Band was formed in 1939 by Frank Walton but, as with many things, the war interfered and he was called up into the RAF in 1941. His talent as a musician stood him in good stead and he was the leader of about eight station bands. Frank retired in 1961 after twenty-three years as leader pianist of the band. Apart from its regular Saturday night stand in the Penrith Drill Hall, it played at numerous dances and social functions in the area. Since its formation the band has had about thirty-seven different players. There were many changes in its early days as the band was affected by the war. Young men had no sooner joined the band than they were called up for service. This photograph, taken in 1955, shows the band with six players, although sometimes there were eight. From left to right: Jack Varty (trumpet), Tommy Arragon (sax), Dick Redhead (drums), Gordon Wilson (sax), Geoff Parr (double bass), leader Frank Walton (piano).

Dancers in the Drill Hall. The Drill Hall was for many years the centre for evening entertainment in Penrith. Many will remember it best for the Saturday night 'bob hops' to the sweet strains of Frank Walton's Melody Makers.

The Penrith Drill Hall was built in Portland Place in 1893 by public subscription at a cost of £3,000. Many functions were held there over the years, such as Saturday night dances, concerts, public meetings, dance bands from London and even a Midget Circus. On 27–29 October 1927 a Grand Bazaar was held there with a view to raising funds for the Conservative Party. It was in the form of Ye Old English Village Fair. The Bill of Fare was Ye Boar's Head, Baron of Beef, Turkey, Capon, Venison, Game Pie, Brawn, York Ham, Tongues, Pastries, Cordials and Trifles. The photograph shows the Drill Hall badly damaged by fire in February 1963. It was later demolished.

SECTION SEVEN
Occasions

A day of celebration for the accession of George V and Queen Mary to the throne in 1910. The dense crowd of well-wishers completely fills Middlegate, which has been decorated with flags and bunting.

Inglewood Rifles officers, 1865. With the passing of Colonel Thomas Machell, it is believed the last link with the popular old 'Skiddaw Greys' has been broken, making the photograph especially interesting. Weekly drills and musters were held in fields opposite the late Mr Rimington's house at Tynefield, and sham fights in Lowther Park. The first man sworn in was William Brougham, later to become Lord Brougham.

Some of the 24th (Cumberland and Westmorland) Company of the Imperial Yeomanry returning to Penrith on Monday 17 June 1901 after serving in the Boer War. The regimental band, mounted guard of Yeomanry, the Town Band under bandmaster James Moffat, the Volunteer Band under bandmaster Riley, and Companies of the Border Regiment headed the procession. At the far end of Middlegate can be seen the Middlegate Brewery, which was pulled down in 1910 to make way for the Alhambra.

The vast crowds gathered around the monument, many hanging from windows, greet the twenty-five Penrith volunteers. Each man was presented with an inscribed gold watch from the people of the town.

The Black Angel. The unveiling ceremony, on 1 March 1906, of the South African War Memorial in Corney Square by General Michael Rimington of Tynefield. The monument, in memory of the men of Penrith and district who fell in the South African War (1899–1902), consists of a large bronze figure with outstretched arms holding a laurel wreath, and stands on an unpolished granite pillar. The capital of the column is very handsomely carved.

During the First World War there were three military hospitals in Penrith, at the Methodist church, St Andrew's parish rooms, and Skiddaw Grove, Lowther Street. The first photograph shows Penrithian Mr Reuben Robson, a member of the VAD, with five convalescing soldiers at Skiddaw Grove. Volunteer Aid Detachments were set up in the area in 1910. Members were mobilized when war was declared to organize hospitals such as the one at Skiddaw Grove. The first wounded arrived there in 1915.

This rare photograph shows wounded soldiers feeding pet lambs in Market Square.

Another rare photograph, showing the donkey and cart which was used to transport those wounded soldiers who were unable to walk around the town. Above the cart, on the wall of No. 19 Devonshire Street, can be seen the sign 'Prince Charlie's Cafe and Temperance Hotel'. It was here that Prince Charles Edward Stuart, Bonnie Prince Charlie, stayed on the night of 22 November 1745 on his journey south.

Horse-drawn ambulances in Castlegate head for the railway station to collect and transport wounded soldiers to the three military hospitals in the town during the First World War.

The cycle section of the Border Volunteer Regiment, probably at Lowther in 1905.

Crowds of well-wishers flank the streets as the Territorials, locally known as the 'Terriers', having left the Drill Hall, march off to the railway station to begin their journey to the war front. Boaters appear to have been very popular with the menfolk.

A crowded platform at Penrith station in 1914, as friends and relatives bid farwell to the young men of the Territorial Army, many of whom would never return.

Old soldiers making the annual pilgrimage to the War Memorial at the Castle Park on 11 November 1934. The procession marched from the Drill Hall, led by the Sons of Temperance Band. Leading the wreath-laying ceremony are Mr J. Nanson, standard bearer, Mr Fred Sayer of The Luham, Edenhall, who was badly injured in the war, Sydney Barron, Anthony Lowther, Chairman of the British Legion, Captain Kidd, and Lady Mabel Howard.

Parading through the town in their dress uniform and led by their own band are the men of one of many regiments who camped in Lowther Park over the years. They are seen here passing the grocers shop of I.G. Sim at the bottom of Brunswick Road, *c.* 1938.

Unsung heroes of the home front: members of Penrith Home Guard led by the Town Band during a wartime parade in 1941.

The visit of the Prince of Wales. On Friday 1 July 1927 the Prince of Wales, later to reign briefly as Edward VIII, received an enthusiastic reception in Penrith: his visit lasted only twenty minutes. Council Chairman Isaac Sim greeted the royal visitor and he is seen here on the Town Hall steps introducing the Prince to councillors and officials. George Wainwright was given pride of place because of his remarkable record of having served local government in the town for forty-four years.

The Prince reviewing the guard of honour provided by the 4th Battalion of the Border Regiment.

Children at Brunswick Road Infants' School await the arrival of the Prince of Wales on his way out of town for a tour of the Lake District.

Some of the congregation boarding a horse-drawn coach after the service at Wythburn church, Thirlmere, with Helvellyn in the background. The Prince of Wales made an unusual stop here on his Lakes tour to inspect a special guard of honour, a group of ten Herdwick rams belonging to Isaac Thompson of West End Farm. The Blencathra Foxhounds outside the church were also seen by the Prince.

Members of the Penrith branch of the British Legion at the railway station in 1938. They were on their way to Newcastle to take part in a large parade of about 15,000 marchers.

The old egg-packing station on Meeting House Lane goes up in flames just after the Second World War. It had been Milburn's cycle and motor-cycle repair shop. One of Penrith's first schools, a day and Sunday school for the Wesleyans, was built here early in the nineteenth century. Penrith's first nonconformist place of worship, the Friends' Meeting House, built in 1701, is just visible on the right.

Frank Keiser and some of his enthusiastic helpers, seen here working on a wing section in 1934, were busy building a glider in rooms above what was Ryan's old lodging house in Princess Street.

The glider is completed, and many willing hands are helping to push it up a fellside near Troutbeck from where it could be launched. Another launching place was Knock Pike, near Appleby.

Marathon walker. Schoolchildren greet Dr Barbara Moore as she passes through Penrith on one of her long walks from Land's End to John O'Groats in 1959. By the time she had completed her last big walk over the same route in 1963, when she was 59, she had walked almost 23,000 miles in the space of four years in places as far away as the United States and Australia. She lived on a diet of fruit, vegetables, juices, nuts, and even grass from roadside verges if there was nothing else! The author's daughters, Helen and Rosemary, are walking close to Dr Moore.

Drivers in the *Daily Express* National Motor Rally take a short rest at the Penrith checkpoint in Great Dockray in November 1952 after their run from Glasgow.

Local enthusiast Graham Howe, with his MGTC and co-driver John Robinson, participants in the rally, before the next leg of the journey south through the Lake District to Wales.

The First Company of Penrith Girl Guides put on a popular play in Christ Church Parish Rooms in 1938.

The Middy Concert Party, run by the Co-operative Society, was a big attraction in 1940.

Compared with the village weddings of the beginning of the century, the 'wedding of the year' in 1960, at St Andrew's church, Penrith, was a very lavish and splendid affair between Mr Robert Edmund Sangster, 24-year-old son of the Vernon Football Pools chief, and Miss Christine Street, daughter of Mr and Mrs F.H.H. Street of the George Hotel, Penrith. Crowds thronged Devonshire Street and the Market Square to see the arrival of the 300 guests, including many distinguished personages. A huge marquee had been erected at Rampsbeck Hotel by the shores of Ullswater to which guests were transported to be received by the bride and groom. The day ended with a dance at the George Hotel. This photograph shows part of the crowd eagerly awaiting the arrival of the bride. Were you there?

The five bridesmaids arrive.

The bride and groom after their marriage.

The big annual event for the residents of Castletown 'ower t'brig' is the crowning of the new queen. The happy day always starts with a procession of children in fancy dress, seen here as it moves off into Alexandra Road.

Some of the prize winners in the fancy dress, first prize going to the 'Scotch thistle'.

Marie Thornley with her attendants after being crowned Queen of Castletown in 1958.

SECTION EIGHT
Transport

Photographed around 1910, this Thornycroft motor bus has just arrived at the top of Kirkstone Pass after the steep climb from Patterdale. The landlord of the inn at that time was Michael Black.

Ready to move off with his four-in-hand, the driver of the wagonette has paused by the ruined castle wall, close to the Garden Nurseries of Joseph Tremble and Son around the turn of the century. It is thought that the house in the castle grounds may have been the residence of the owners.

On a wet day, and with a full complement of passengers, top-hatted driver George Henry Eland is ready to leave, *c.* 1906. He was employed by the Crown Hotel for many years, having charge of the four-in-hand which plied between the town and Pooley Bridge. Mr Eland died in 1941 aged 59.

Off to Ullswater. One of Penrith's earliest charabancs is about to leave the Station Hotel, Castlegate, for a trip around the lakes, *c.* 1910. Solid-tyred, chain-driven, and with a top speed of 12 m.p.h., AO545 was a Durham Churchill purchased in 1907 by the Penrith and District Motor Services. After a few years it was taken over by the owners of the Ullswater steamers, along with two other charas. During the First World War all three vehicles were requisitioned for war work and converted into flat lorries. After the war AO545 returned to Penrith, where it was purchased by Armstrong & Siddle who continued to run it as a lorry until 1920.

AO545, driven by Tom Fleming, arrives in Langwathby in 1908 on its regular twice-weekly run to Apppleby (on Tuesdays and Saturdays). The little boy in the wide-brimmed hat is Mr Watson Spark of The Mains, Stainton. Mr Spark, now a retired farmer, was with his late sister Mary and his father and mother, George and Mary Spark, who farmed Scaws Farm, Penrith. In 1906, 7,400 passengers were carried on Penrith and District Motor Service buses.

One of Penrith's earliest cars, photographed in 1910. Chauffeur Robert Watson is at the wheel of Dr Robert Bathgate Johnstone's 10/12 hp 'Swift', a 2-seater car painted dark green and weighing 12 cwt. Described as a physician and surgeon, he was the medical officer of Westmorland. Presumably he was associated with the Thomson family who practised medicine in Bishop Yards. Who owned Penrith's first car? It is impossible to be sure as registration numbers were only issued by Cumberland County Council from 4 December 1903. It is fairly certain, however, that a 6 hp Light Wolsely, jointly owned by Dr Joseph Edward Bowser and Dr John Livingstone and purchased in 1899, was the first, although it is often said that the late Mr J.E. Irving of Rawcroft, Arthur Street, was the first car owner in town. Certainly he was the most prolific; he is said to have owned at least twenty-five cars.

Some of the Simonini family and a friend in their Model T Ford, with the ruins of Penrith Castle in the background, in the early 1920s.

A line up of T Ford cars outside the garage of Tinkler & Co., Victoria Road, in 1924. Tinkler's were agents for Ford cars at that time. In the driving seat of the first car is Mr William Morris of Morris Motors. He had driven up in one of his cars through England and Scotland for exhibition purposes, possibly seeking agents to sell the vehicle.

Having a pleasant afternoon out are Miss Hilda Sim, at the wheel of her Austin Seven, her elder sister Mrs Hannah McLean, and friend Miss Ann Sayer, later Mrs Johnstone. Miss Sim had a toy shop in the Cornmarket for many years and Miss Sayer kept the baby linen shop nearby. They are parked here on Martindale Hause, looking down on Howtown Hotel, c. 1930.

Penrith's first two AA patrolmen in the early 1930s with their mode of transport of that time, motor-bikes and sidecars. On the right is Mr Jimmy Fisher, centre is Billy Lightfoot and a visiting inspector is left.

The chimney at the former Glasson's brewery was brought down on 5 November 1967. The brewery, built in 1857, was being demolished to allow extension of the Roper Street Garage.

Mr Ernie Hartness was the pioneer of the longest lasting private bus service in Penrith. He started in 1917 with horses and carriages, transferring in 1922 to an early Daimler which had seen service in the First World War. It had a removable bus body on its lorry platform and solid tyres. This bus, seen here with Mr Hartness in the cab, was the forerunner of his eventual fleet of forty-three buses.

The entrance to the new bus station in Sandgate in the 1950s, with a Daimler coach of the type with which the fleet was to be standardized. On the right are Ernie and Billy Douglas. Billy was goalkeeper for the Penrith football team for many years.

Mr Hartness ran buses for the Football Supporters Club to away matches in the Northern League. On this occasion the Penrith club had a large following, possibly to a cup match. Twelve buses are taking fans to County Durham. In the background can be seen Glasson's Brewery and chimney. This Penrith landmark was demolished along with the brewery in November 1967.

In 1935 Tom Parkinson ran the Ship Hotel. In the doorway stands Joe Robinson, a driver and nephew of Mr Hartness. The hotel was used as a Carriers Quarters for the Skelton bus service, performing this service from 1917 when it began with horses and carriages.

A tight squeeze for a big load. A huge casting for a ship's stern, 19 ft 6 in wide and weighing 20 tons, passed through Penrith on 8 March 1953 en route from Glasgow to Middlesbrough. It is seen here descending Castlegate. Before the motorway was built many massive loads like this one passed through the town and because of their width could not negotiate the 'narrows' between Devonshire Street and Middlegate so had to be diverted via Brunswick Road, Cromwell Road and Castlegate. The bottleneck locally known as 'Arnison's Narrows' at 11 ft 6 in wide is the narrowest street anywhere on the north-west road between England and Scotland.

A large boiler negotiates the corner on its descent of Castlegate.

'If Britain can make it, Pickfords can take it', says the slogan. This large cylindrical container, 130 ft long, is making its way from Stockton-on-Tees to a BP oil refinery in Glasgow on 29 June 1958. It is seen here about to negotiate Arnison's famous 'narrows' and is attracting a great deal of attention.

A rail accident of nearly 100 years ago. This fatal accident occurred in Penrith station on 5 December 1903, when a goods wagon broke loose from a train at Shap, ran back, and collided with the south-bound sleeper-mail train pulled by LNWR locomotive 1665 *Dagmar*. The driver, Mr Bates, was thrown out onto the platform and killed. This shows the badly damaged engine.

Sightseers on the platform examine the derailed coaches.

Engine men of the North Eastern Railway who worked the trains from Penrith over the hazardous Stainmore route – often blocked by snow in winter – to Darlington in the yard at Penrith in the early 1920s. The engine depicted is an NER 2–4–0 (901 class). This, the last of Edward Fletcher's experimental classes, had 7 ft driving wheels and fifty-five were built between 1872 and 1882. There was not much protection in the cab of this class of locomotive for the foot-plate crew over the bleak Stainmore. Like many other lines, this one, opened in 1862, did not miss the Beeching axe in the 1960s, and on Saturday 20 January 1962 the last train ran over Stainmore.

Jumbo 25050 *Merrie Carlisle* and its partner *Snowdon* were both shedded at Penrith and for many years worked local trains to Carlisle and Workington. Here the former, with driver Steve Bamber and fireman David Pattinson, prepares to move out of the Myers siding into the station with the 8 a.m. 'workmans' train to Carlisle. Both engines were withdrawn in 1934 to be broken up after sixty years of service.

The blue and silver, streamlined *Coronation Scot* makes a striking picture as it speeds south through Penrith under threatening skies on a June afternoon in 1938.

The hard winter of 1940/1. A Fowler 4F 4009 equipped with snow plough waits at Penruddock, with driver Joe Dalton and fireman John Nattrass in charge, before proceeding to clear the line to Keswick blocked at St Andrew's cutting.

No. 4009 well and truly buried in the cutting it came to clear. Behind it, a 'Cauliflower' that came to the rescue – also trapped in the snow.

Three Penrith railwaymen in the steam days of the 1950s: driver Joe Dalton, guard George Walker and driver Steve Bamber. (Note the bottle of cold tea in Steve's pocket.)

Rebuilt Scot 46126 *Royal Army Service Corps* coasts into Penrith with a West Coast special and a full head of steam after a 12 mile run down from Shap summit in 1964. Significant in the picture is the 50 ft tall co-acting signal; these were necessary at Penrith because of the very sharp curve through the station.

Penrith No. 2 box. Signalman Arthur Jackson has a quick word with the driver of Ivatt 46432 as it heads out to Keswick with the Workington portion of the 'Lakes Express' on 29 August 1964. The single line working tablet would be picked up at No. 1 box further along the line. The Cockermouth, Keswick and Penrith line, opened in January 1865, was yet another victim of the Beeching cutback and was finally closed on 4 March 1972.

Spring water descending from the banks above the River Eamont has frozen, forming these massive icicles near Honeypot Farm, Edenhall, during the long hard winter of 1947.

Acknowledgements

The author is pleased to acknowledge the invaluable help which has been kindly given by the following people who have lent photographs and supplied information.

Mrs D. Airey • Mrs J. Brown • Mr C. Butterworth • Mrs M. Clark • Mr J. Clement • Mrs M. Cragg • Mr P. Crowden • Mr F. Dalton • Mr R. Dearden Mr K. Elliott • Mrs B. Fawcett • Mr A. Fraser • Mr D. Fallowfield • Mr D. Goulding • Mr O. Harrison • Mrs M. Horn • Mr G. Hodgson • Mr J Hurst Mrs J.D. London • Mr G. Lancaster • Mrs K.M. Kidd • Mrs E. Main • Mr E. Merrie • Mrs W.F. Mounsey • Mrs E. Pounder • Mrs O. Rawes • Mr M. Robson • Mrs D. Ryelands • Mr A. Simonini • Mr F. Walton • Mrs S. Wallace Mr H. Wishart

Special thanks go to my cousin Mrs Bertha Mitchinson, Mrs Judith Clarke of the Penrith Museum, my daughter Mrs Helen Baines, and my wife Mary.

Errors and omissions are entirely the responsibility of the author.

Penrith is a very historic town. The former capital of Cumbria, it has at times formed part of the kingdom of Scotland. It is a lot more tranquil these days, enjoying a measure of prosperity as a flourishing market town of charm and beauty, but it has seen a fair number of changes in the hundred years since the use of photography became widespread.

As well as numerous historic views of the Market Place and of the streets of the town, however, this selection includes sections on the people of Penrith as they have traditionally gone about their work and leisure, or celebrated special occasions. They are not what the tourists come to see but they are the heroes of this book.

Frank Boyd is a life-long resident of Penrith who acquired a camera in 1934 and has been taking photographs of the town ever since. When his own work acquired the patina of age he began to take an interest in other early views of the town, and the results of his collecting efforts are presented here for historians professional and amateur and for those who simply enjoy a ramble down memory lane.

£7.99

ALAN SUTTON PUBLISHING
PHOENIX MILL . STROUD
GLOUCESTERSHIRE

ISBN 0-7509-0281-7

9 780750 902816